40 Hadith on Sufism

Sheikh Abu Abd Al Rahman Al Sulami

*The day when neither wealth nor
children will avail, except him who
comes to God with a heart that
is sound. And Paradise will be
brought near for the God-fearing.*

Al-Shu'ara, 26:88-90

Contents

In the Name of Allah, the Compassionate, the Merciful;
May Allah bless our Master Muhammad
and grant him peace.

Translator's Introduction

Sheikh Abu Abd al-Rahman al-Sulami (325–412 AH) was the undisputed sheikh of Sufism in Khorasan during his lifetime. He authored 700 volumes on Sufism and 300 in Hadith, in addition to works in Tafsir and other disciplines. A man who bore the markings of Divine acceptance, he was loved by common men and princes, yet politely declined the extravagant gifts of the latter. His works were so popular that swaths of people would gather to listen to his public readings and lectures.

Among his works is a compilation of 40 hadiths on the subject of Sufism—spirituality in Islam—with his own chains of transmission returning to the Prophet ﷺ, his companions, or the generation after them. Imam al-Sakhawi (831–902 AH), one of the erudite luminaries of Hadith science, produced a derivative work (known as a *takhrij*) in which he checked and graded al-Sulami's collection. He also provided corroborating transmissions (*shawahid*). While not all of the hadiths in al-Sulami's collection are authentic, the principles they demonstrate are, without doubt, central to Sufism, and, consequently, compliant with the noble Sharia. True Sufism is the spiritual dimension of Islamic Law. Anything that contradicts the Law is either fraud or misguidance.

In addition to the translation of Sheikh al-Sulami's collection of 40 hadiths on Sufism, brief footnotes—gleaned and paraphrased from Imam al-Sakhawi's derivative text—are included in the following work.

Translation is interpretation, and, given the cultural, temporal, and linguistic gaps between the original and what is herein presented, interpretation is very much necessary. (In the case of the last entry in the collection in particular, the verses of Arabic poetry are translated artistically—metre, rhyme, and beauty are prioritized over accuracy.) The original Arabic is placed alongside the English not only because there are spiritual and linguistic benefits in reading it, but also to allow those with access to scholars to gain a deeper understanding and appreciation of the Sunnah.

May Allah bless this work, guide us, and mostly, forgive us; ameen.

Moustafa Elqabbany
November 2015 | Muharram 1437

Imam al-Sakhawi's Chain of Transmission for the Text

The Sheikh of Islam and Master of our Age, Abu al-Fadl Ahmad ibn Hajar (may Allah have mercy upon him) apprised me, having read with Abu al-Hasan Ali ibn Muhammad ibn Muhammad ibn Abu al-Majd, who said that Abu al-Fath Muhammad ibn Abd al-Rahim ibn al-Nashw informed us with authorization that Abu Muhammad Abd al-Wahhab ibn Dhafir ibn Rawwaj apprised us that al-Hafidh Abu Tahir Ahmad ibn Muhammad ibn Ahmad al-Silafi apprised us that Abu al-Tayyib Tahir ibn al-Musaddad al-Janazi apprised us that Abu al-Hasan Ali ibn Abd al-Rahman al-Naysabouri apprised us that Abu Abd al-Rahman ibn al-Husayn al-Sulami (may Allah have mercy upon him) apprised us, saying:

إِسْنَادُ الْإِمَامِ السَّخَاوِيِّ فِي الْكِتَابِ

أخبرني شيخ الإسلام حافظ العصر أبو الفضل أحمد بن حجر رحمه الله، عن أبي الحسن علي بن محمد بن محمد ابن أبي المجد قراءة، قال: أنبأنا أبو الفتح محمد بن عبد الرحيم بن النشو إجازة: أخبرنا أبو محمد عبد الوهاب ابن ظافر بن رواج: أخبرنا الحافظ أبو طاهر أحمد بن محمد بن أحمد السلفي: أخبرنا أبو الطيب طاهر بن المسدد الجنزي: أخبرنا أبو الحسن علي ابن عبد الرحمن النيسابوري: أخبرنا أبو عبد الرحمن محمد بن الحسين السلمي رحمه الله، قال:

1. Proof that Sufis are the Companions of the Messenger of Allah ﷺ

Muhammad ibn Muhammad ibn Sa'id al-Anmati apprised us that al-Hasan ibn Ali ibn Yahya ibn Sallam told us that Muhammad ibn Ali al-Tirmidhi told us that Sa'id ibn Hatim al-Balkhi told us that Sahl ibn Aslam told us, on the authority of Khallad ibn Muhammad, on the authority of Abu Hamza al-Sukkari, on the authority of Yazid al-Nahwi, on the authority of Ikrima, on the authority of Ibn Abbas 🙪, who said:

The Messenger of Allah ﷺ stood before the People of al-Suffah[1] one day, and, seeing their neediness, strain, and the goodness of their hearts, said, "Rejoice, O People of al-Suffah! Whosoever of my nation remains in the state you are in, content with it, will be among my companions on the Day of Resurrection."

---

1 Al-Suffah was a shaded area at the rear of the mosque in Medina where destitute emigrants, lacking family and wealth, would stay.

١. بَابُ الدَّلِيلِ عَلَى أَنَّ الصُّوفِيَّةَ هُمْ رُفَقَاءُ رَسُولِ الله ﷺ

أخبرنا محمد بن محمد بن سعيد الأنماطي: حدثنا الحسن بن علي بن يحيى بن سلَّام: حدثنا محمد بن علي الترمذي: حدثنا سعيد بن حاتم البلخي: حدثنا سهل بن أسلم، عن خلَّاد بن محمد، عن أبي حمزة السُّكَّري، عن يزيد النحوي، عن عكرمة، عن ابن عباس ﵁ قال:

وَقَفَ رَسُولُ الله ﷺ يوماً عَلَى أَصْحَابِ الصُّفَّةِ، فَرَأَى فَقْرَهُمْ، وَجُهْدَهُمْ، وَطِيبَ قُلُوبِهِمْ، فَقَالَ: «أَبْشِرُوا يَا أَصْحَابَ الصُّفَّةِ! مَنْ بَقِيَ مِنْ أُمَّتِي عَلَى النَّعْتِ الَّذِي أَنْتُمْ عَلَيْهِ، رَاضِياً بِمَا فِيهِ، فَإِنَّهُ مِنْ رُفَقَائِي يَوْمَ القِيَامَةِ».

2. The Manner of Fakirs

Abu al-Qasim Abd al-Rahman ibn Ahmad ibn Mattawayh al-Balkhi apprised us that Fahdi ibn Jasnasfanna told us that Muhammad ibn Isma'il al-Ahmasi told us that Uthman ibn Abd al-Rahman al-Harrani told us that al-Wazi' ibn Nafi' told us, on the authority of Abu Salama, on the authority of Thawban ﷺ who said:

The Messenger of Allah ﷺ said, "My cistern spans the distance between Aden and Amman. Its drink is whiter than milk and sweeter than honey. Whoever drinks a single draught from it will never again feel thirsty. The first to arrive at it are the destitute Emigrants." We asked, "Who are they, O Messenger of Allah?" He said, "Those of dingy raiment and dusty, unkempt hair, for whom gates are not opened and who are not given pampered women in marriage; those who fulfill their duties and do not receive their due. Then people will appear who say, 'I am so-and-so, son of so-and-so', and I will say, 'You have altered matters after me.'"[1]

---

[1] It was also narrated by: al-Tirmidhi, Ibn Majah, Ahmad, al-Bayhaqi in *al-Ba'th*, and al-Hakim in *al-Mustadrak*, who said, "It has a sound chain of narrators, but they [(i.e. Bukhari and Muslim)] did not narrate it." Muslim narrated it as well in a different context.

٢. بابٌ في صِفةِ الْفُقَرَاءِ

أخبرنا أبو القاسم عبد الرحمن بن أحمد بن مَتَّوَيْهِ البَلْخِي: حدثنا فَهْدِي بن جَسْنَسْفَنَّة: حدثنا محمد بن إسماعيل الأَحْمَسي: حدثنا عثمان بن عبد الرحمن الحَرَّاني: حدثنا الوازع بن نافع، عن أبي سلمة، عن ثوبان ﷺ قال:

قَالَ رَسُولُ الله ﷺ: «حَوْضِي مَا بَيْنَ عَدَنَ إِلَى عَمَّانَ. شَرَابُهُ أَبْيَضُ مِنَ اللَّبَنِ، وَأَحْلَى مِنَ الْعَسَلِ. مَنْ شَرِبَ مِنْهُ شَرْبَةً لَا يَظْمَأُ بَعْدَهَا أَبَداً. وَأَوَّلُ مَنْ يَرِدُهُ صَعَالِيكُ الْمُهَاجِرِينَ». قُلنا: وَمَنْ هُمْ يَا رَسُولَ الله؟ قَالَ: «الدُّنْسُ الثِّيَابِ، الشُّعْثُ الرُّؤُوسِ، الَّذِينَ لَا تُفْتَحُ لَهُمْ أَبْوَابُ السُّدَدِ، وَلَا يُزَوَّجُونَ الْمُنَعَّمَاتِ، الَّذِينَ يُعْطُونَ مَا عَلَيْهِمْ، وَلَا يُعْطَوْنَ مَا لَهُمْ، وَلَيَأْتِيَنَّ أَقْوَامٌ فَيَقُولُونَ: أَنَا فُلَانُ بْنُ فُلَانٍ، وَلَأَقُولَنَّ: إِنَّكُمْ بَدَّلْتُمْ بَعْدِي».¹

---

١ رواه الترمذي وابن ماجه وأحمد والبيهقي في البعث والحاكم في المستدرك، وقال: «إنه صحيح الإسناد ولم يخرجاه». ورواه مسلم بسياق أخرى.

3. Maintaining Good Conduct Even with Disbelievers

Zahir ibn Ahmad al-Faqih apprised us that Ali ibn Muhammad ibn al-Faraj al-Ahwazi told us that Sulayman ibn al-Rabi' al-Khazzaz told us that Kadih ibn Rahmah told us, on the authority of Abu Umayyah ibn Ya'la, on the authority of Sa'id ibn Abu Sa'id, on the authority of Abu Hurayra ﷺ who said:

The Messenger of Allah ﷺ said: "Allah ﷻ revealed to Abraham ﷺ: 'You are my beloved friend. Make good your conduct even with disbelievers and you will enter the abodes of the reverent, for I have already decreed that whosoever makes good his conduct, I shall shade him under My throne, settle him in My sacred enclosure, and bring him nigh unto My proximity.'"

٣. بَابُ اسْتِعْمَالِ الخُلُقِ وَلَوْ مَعَ الكُفَّارِ

أخبرنا زاهر بن أحمد الفقيه: حدثنا علي بن محمد بن الفرج الأهوازي: حدثنا سليمان بن الربيع الخَزَّاز: حدثنا كادح بن رحمة، عن أبي أمية بن يعلى، عن سعيد بن أبي سعيد، عن أبي هريرة ﷺ قال:

قَالَ رَسُولُ اللهِ ﷺ: «أَوْحَى اللهُ ﷻ إِلَى إِبْرَاهِيمَ ﷺ: إِنَّكَ خَلِيلِي، حَسِّنْ خُلُقَكَ وَلَوْ مَعَ الكُفَّارِ، تَدْخُلْ مَدَاخِلَ الأَبْرَارِ، فَإِنَّ كَلِمَتِي سَبَقَتْ لِمَنْ حَسَّنَ خُلُقَهُ أَنْ أُظِلَّهُ تَحْتَ عَرْشِي، وَأُسْكِنَهُ حَظِيرَةَ قُدْسِي، وَأُدْنِيَهُ مِنْ جِوَارِي».

11

4. Those Who Give Up All of Their Wealth Out of Trust in Allah ﷻ

Abu al-Hasan Muhammad ibn Muhammad ibn al-Hasan ibn al-Harith al-Karazi apprised us that Ali ibn Abd al-Aziz apprised us that Abu Nu'aym al-Fadl ibn Dukayn told us that Hisham ibn Saad told us, on the authority of Zayd ibn Aslam, on the authority of his father, who said:

I heard Umar say, "The Messenger of Allah ﷺ ordered us to give in charity at a time when I had wealth in my possession. I said, 'If I am going to outstrip Abu Bakr, it will be today.' I came with half of my wealth and the Messenger of Allah ﷺ asked, 'What did you leave for your family?' I said, 'Its equivalent.' Abu Bakr then came with everything in his possession, and he [i.e. the Messenger] asked, 'O Abu Bakr, what did you leave for your family?' He replied, 'Allah and His Messenger.' I said, 'I will never vie with you for anything.'" [1]

---

1   It was also narrated by: Abu Dawud, al-Tirmidhi (who said, "This is a good, authentic hadith"), and al-Hakim in *al-Mustadrak* (who said after it, "This is an authentic hadith according to Muslim's criteria, but they did not narrate it.").

٤ . بابٌ فِيمَنْ تَخَلَّى مِنْ جَمِيعِ مَالِهِ ثِقَةً بِاللهِ ﷻ

أخبرنا أبو الحسن محمد بن محمد بن الحسن بن الحارث الكارزي: أخبرنا علي بن عبد العزيز: حدثنا أبو نُعَيم الفضل بن دُكَين: حدثنا هشام بن سعد، عن زيد بن أسلم، عن أبيه، قال:

سَمِعْتُ عُمَرَ يَقُولُ: أَمَرَنَا رَسُولُ اللهِ ﷺ أَنْ نَتَصَدَّقَ فَوَافَقَ ذَلِكَ مَالاً كَانَ عِنْدِي، فَقُلْتُ: الْيَوْمَ أَسْبِقُ أَبَا بَكْرٍ إِنْ سَبَقْتُهُ، فَجِئْتُ بِنِصْفِ مَالِي، فَقَالَ رَسُولُ اللهِ ﷺ: «مَاذَا أَبْقَيْتَ لِأَهْلِكَ»؟ قُلْتُ: مِثْلَهُ. وَأَتَى أَبُو بَكْرٍ بِكُلِّ مَا عِنْدَهُ، فَقَالَ: «يَا أَبَا بَكْرٍ، مَاذَا أَبْقَيْتَ لِأَهْلِكَ»؟ قَالَ: اللهَ وَرَسُولَهُ. قُلْتُ: لَا أُسَابِقُكَ إِلَى شَيْءٍ أَبَداً.[1]

---

[1] رواه أبو داود والترمذي، وقال: «هذا حديث حسن صحيح»، والحاكم في المستدرك، وقال عقبه: «هذا حديث صحيح على شرط مسلم، ولم يخرجاه».

13

5. The Admissibility of Miracles at the Hands of Saints

Muhammad ibn Muhammad ibn Ya'qub al-Hafidh apprised us that Ahmad ibn Abd al-Warith ibn Jarir al-Assal told us in Egypt that al-Harith ibn Miskeen apprised us that Ibn Wahb apprised us that Yahya ibn Ayyub apprised me, on the authority of Ibn Ajlan, on the authority of Nafi', on the authority of Ibn Umar:

> Umar ﷺ dispatched an army and put in charge of it a man known as "Sariya". Later, while delivering a sermon, Umar began to shout, "O Sariya, the mountain! O Sariya, the mountain!" Then an emissary from the army arrived and said, "O Commander of the Faithful, we faced our enemy and they defeated us when, all of a sudden, a voice cried out, 'O Sariya, the mountain!', so we backed ourselves against the mountain and Allah the Exalted defeated them." We said to Umar, "You were yelling it."

Ibn Ajlan said, "Iyas ibn Mu'awiyah ibn Qurra [also] told me [this]."[1]

---

1 Al-Bayhaqi also narrated it in *Dala'il al-Nubuwwa*. Al-Sakhawi said, "This is a good chain of narrators."

٥. بَابٌ فِي جَوَازِ الْكَرَامَاتِ لِلْأَوْلِيَاءِ

أخبرنا محمد بن محمد بن يعقوب الحافظ: حدثنا أحمد بن عبد الوارث ابن جرير العسّال بمصر: أخبرنا الحارث بن مسكين: أخبرنا ابن وَهْب: أخبرني يحيى بن أيوب، عن ابن عجلان، عن نافع، عن ابن عمر:

أَنَّ عُمَرَ ﷺ بَعَثَ جَيْشاً، فَأَمَّرَ عَلَيْهِمْ رَجُلاً يُدْعَى سَارِيَةَ، فَبَيْنَمَا عُمَرُ يَخْطُبُ فَجَعَلَ يَصِيحُ: يَا سَارِيَةُ الْجَبَلَ، يَا سَارِيَةُ الْجَبَلَ، فَقَدِمَ رَسُولٌ مِنَ الْجَيْشِ، فَقَالَ: يَا أَمِيرَ الْمُؤْمِنِينَ، لَقِينَا عَدُوَّنَا فَهَزَمُونَا، فَإِذَا صَائِحٌ يَصِيحُ يَا سَارِيَةُ الْجَبَلَ، فَأَسْنَدْنَا ظُهُورَنَا إِلَى الْجَبَلِ، فَهَزَمَهُمُ اللهُ تَعَالَى، فَقُلْنَا لِعُمَرَ: كُنْتَ تَصِيحُ بِذَلِكَ.

قال ابن عجلان: وحدثني إياس بن معاوية بن قُرَّة.[1]

---

[1] ورواه البيهقي في الدلائل، وقال السخاوي: «وهو إسناد حسن».

The Admissibility of Miracles
at the Hands of Saints (...)

Umar ibn Ahmad ibn Uthman ibn Shahin apprised us that Abdullah ibn Sulayman ibn al-Ash'ath told us that Ayyub ibn Muhammad al-Wazzan told us that Khattab ibn Salama al-Mousili told us that Umar ibn Abu al-Azhar told us, on the authority of Malik ibn Anas, on the authority of Nafi', on the authority of Ibn Umar:

Umar ﷺ delivered a sermon in Medina one day and said, "O Sariya, the mountain! Whosoever places a wolf in charge of a flock has wronged it.[1]" Someone noted, "He mentions Sariya while Sariya is in Iraq." People told Ali ﷺ, "Did you not hear of the one who said 'O Sariya' while delivering a sermon on the pulpit?" He said, "Woe unto you! Leave Umar alone, for he does not get himself into something without getting himself out of it." Only a short time passed until Sariya arrived and said, "I heard Umar's voice and then climbed the mountain."

---

1   A wolf put in charge of a flock bears a burden that it cannot be expected to handle, and is therefore oppressed. The "wolf" in this context is the enemy army. Umar ﷺ thus warned Sariya against giving the enemy an easy victory because they would necessarily attack the compromised Muslim army as a wolf attacks a flock. Other versions and interpretations exist, and Allah knows best.

بَابٌ فِي جَوَازِ الْكَرَامَاتِ لِلْأَوْلِيَاءِ (...)

أخبرنا عمر بن أحمد بن عثمان بن شاهين: حدثنا عبد الله بن سليمان بن الأشعث: حدثنا أيوب بن محمد الوَزَّان: حدثنا خطَّاب بن سلمة الموصلي: حدثنا عمر بن أبي الأزهر، عن مالك بن أنس، عن نافع، عن ابن عمر:

أَنَّ عُمَرَ ﷺ خَطَبَ يَوْماً بِالْمَدِينَةِ فَقَالَ: يَا سَارِيَةُ الْجَبَلَ، مَنِ اسْتَرْعَى الذِّئْبَ فَقَدْ ظَلَمَهُ، فَقِيلَ: يَذْكُرُ السَّارِيَةَ، وَالسَّارِيَةُ بِالْعِرَاقِ، فَقَالَ النَّاسُ لِعَلِيٍّ ﷺ: مَا سَمِعْتَ عَمَّنْ يَقُولُ: يَا سَارِيَةُ وَهُوَ يَخْطُبُ عَلَى الْمِنْبَرِ، فَقَالَ: وَيْحَكُمْ، دَعُوا عُمَرَ، فَإِنَّهُ مَا دَخَلَ فِي شَيْءٍ إِلَّا خَرَجَ مِنْهُ، فَلَمْ يَلْبَثْ إِلَّا يَسِيراً حَتَّى قَدِمَ سَارِيَةُ، فَقَالَ: سَمِعْتُ صَوْتَ عُمَرَ فَصَعِدْتُ الْجَبَلَ.

6. The Use of Noble Manners, Encouragement of Spending, the Blameworthiness of Hoarding, and Avoiding Questionable Matters

Ibrahim ibn Ahmad apprised us that Abu al-Tayyib az-Zarrad al-Manbaji told us that Hilal ibn al-Alaa told us that my father told us that Umar ibn Hafs told us that Hawshab and Matar told us, on the authority of al-Hasan, on the authority of Imran ibn Husoyn, who said:

The Messenger of Allah ﷺ grasped the tail of my turban from behind me and then said, "O Imran! Verily, Allah loves spending and hates stinginess, so eat, feed [others], and do not hoard it [i.e. wealth] greedily lest its acquisition become difficult for you. And realize that Allah loves penetrating vision at the arrival of questionable matters and a perfected mind at the descent of lusts. He loves largesse even if [expressed] through a few dates, and He loves bravery even when killing a serpent."

٦. بابُ اسْتِعْمَالِ مَكَارِمِ الْأَخْلَاقِ وَالْحَثِّ عَلَى الْإِنْفَاقِ، كَرَاهِيَةِ الادِّخَارِ، وَالْوُقُوفِ عِنْدَ الشُّبُهَاتِ

أخبرنا إبراهيمُ بنُ أحمدَ بنِ محمدِ بنِ رجاءٍ: حدثنا أبو الطيبِ الزَّرَّادُ المنبجي: حدثنا هلالُ بنُ العلاءِ: حدثنا عمرُ بنُ حفصٍ: حدثنا حَوْشَبٌ ومطرٌ، عن الحسنِ، عن عمرانَ بنِ حُصَيْنٍ، قال:

أَخَذَ رَسُولُ اللهِ ﷺ بِطَرَفِ عِمَامَتِي مِنْ وَرَائِي، ثُمَّ قَالَ: «يَا عِمْرَانُ، إِنَّ اللهَ يُحِبُّ الْإِنْفَاقَ، وَيُبْغِضُ الْإِقْتَارَ، فَكُلْ وَأَطْعِمْ، وَلَا تَصُرَّهُ صَرًّا فَيَعْسُرَ عَلَيْكَ الطَّلَبُ، وَاعْلَمْ أَنَّ اللهَ يُحِبُّ الْبَصَرَ النَّافِذَ عِنْدَ مَجِيءِ الشُّبُهَاتِ، وَالْعَقْلَ الْكَامِلَ عِنْدَ نُزُولِ الشَّهَوَاتِ، وَيُحِبُّ السَّمَاحَةَ وَلَوْ عَلَى تَمَرَاتٍ، وَيُحِبُّ الشَّجَاعَةَ وَلَوْ عَلَى قَتْلِ حَيَّةٍ».

19

7. The Manner of Believers and Scholars

Ahmad ibn Muhammad al-Qahtab al-Tajir apprised us that Muhammad ibn Ahmad ibn Thawban told us that Muhammad ibn Isma'il al-Sa'igh told us that Abu al-Salt al-Harawi told us that Yousuf ibn Atiyya told us, on the authority of Qatada, on the authority of al-Hasan, on the authority of Anas ﷺ, who said:

The Messenger of Allah ﷺ said, "Faith is not through wishes and embellishments. Rather, it is that which settles in the heart and is ratified by action. And knowledge is of two types: knowledge of the tongue and knowledge of the heart. Knowledge of the heart is what is beneficial whereas knowledge of the tongue is Allah's argument against the Son of Adam."[1]

---

1   It was also narrated by al-Hakeem al-Tirmidhi (not to be confused with Abu Isa al-Tirmidhi, the famous hadith collector) in *Nawadir al-Usool* with the Companion's name omitted. Al-Sakhawi mentions that its chain of narrators is authentic.

٧. بَابٌ فِي صِفَةِ الْمُؤْمِنِينَ وَصِفَةِ الْعُلَمَاءِ

أخبرنا أحمد بن محمد القَحْطَبي التاجر: حدثنا محمد بن أحمد بن ثَوْبان: حدثنا محمد بن إسماعيل الصائغ: حدثنا أبو الصلت الهَرَوي: حدثنا يوسف بن عطية، عن قتادة، عن الحسن، عن أنس ﷺ، قال:

قَالَ رَسُولُ اللهِ ﷺ: «لَيْسَ الْإِيمَانُ بِالتَّمَنِّي وَلَا بِالتَّحَلِّي، وَلَكِنْ مَا وَقَرَ فِي الْقَلْبِ وَصَدَّقَهُ الْعَمَلُ، وَالْعِلْمُ عِلْمَانِ: عِلْمٌ بِاللِّسَانِ، وَعِلْمٌ بِالْقَلْبِ، فَعِلْمُ الْقَلْبِ النَّافِعُ، وَعِلْمُ اللِّسَانِ حُجَّةُ اللهِ عَلَى ابْنِ آدَمَ».١

---

١ ورواه الحكيم الترمذي مرسلا في النوادر، وصحح إسناده السخاوي.

8. Being Satisfied with the Bare Minimum of Worldly Matters and the Reprehensibility of Mingling with the Affluent

Ibrahim ibn Ahmad ibn Muhammad al-Buzari apprised us that al-Hasan ibn Sufyan apprised us that Makhlad ibn Muhammad told us that Sa'id ibn Muhammad al-Warraq told us, on the authority of Salih ibn Hassan al-Ansari, on the authority of Urwa, on the authority of Aisha 🙵, who said:

The Messenger of Allah 🙵 said, "If you desire to keep close to me, then let the provision of a rider suffice you, and beware of mingling with the affluent."

٨. بَابٌ فِي الِاكْتِفَاءِ مِنَ الدُّنْيَا بِأَقَلِّ الْقَلِيلِ وَكَرَاهِيَةِ مُخَالَطَةِ الْأَغْنِيَاءِ

أَخبرنا إِبراهيم بن أحمد بن محمد البُزَاري: أخبرنا الحسن بن سفيان: حدثنا مَخْلَد بن محمد: حدثنا سعيد بن محمد الوَرَّاق: عن صالح بن حسان الأنصاريّ، عن عروة، عن عائشة ﵂، قالت:

قَالَ رَسُولُ اللهِ ﷺ: «إِنْ أَرَدْتِ اللُّحُوقَ بِي فَلْيَكْفِكِ مِنَ الدُّنْيَا بِقَدْرِ زَادِ الرَّاكِبِ، وَإِيَّاكِ وَمُخَالَطَةَ الْأَغْنِيَاءِ».

23

9. Contentment

Abu al-Abbas Muhammad ibn Ya'qub al-Asamm apprised us that al-Rabi' ibn Sulayman told us that Asad ibn Musa told us that Abu Bakr al-Dahiri told us that Thawr ibn Yazid told us, on the authority of Khalid ibn Muhajir, on the authority of Ibn Umar 🕮, who said:

The Messenger of Allah 🕮 said, "O Son of Adam, you have what suffices you yet you desire what corrupts you. O Son of Adam, you are neither content with little nor sated by plenty. If you reach morning sound in body, secure in route and property, and with your day's supply of food, then may the world be forgotten.[1]"[2]

---

1   i.e. Beyond basic needs, the world is but a digression.
2   After indicating the narration's weakness, al-Sakhawi added, "However, this hadith has corroborating narrations."

٩. بابٌ في الْقَنَاعَة

أخبرنا أبو العباس محمد بن يعقوب الأصمّ: حدثنا الربيع بن سليمان: حدثنا أسد بن موسى: حدثنا أبو بكر الدّاهري: حدثنا ثور بن يزيد، عن خالد بن مهاجر، عن ابن عمر ﵄، قال:

قَالَ رَسُولُ الله ﷺ: «ابْنَ آدَمَ! عِنْدَكَ مَا يَكْفِيكَ، وَأَنْتَ تَطْلُبُ مَا يُطْغِيكَ. ابْنَ آدَمَ! لَا بِقَلِيلٍ تَقْنَعُ، وَلَا مِنْ كَثِيرٍ تَشْبَعُ، إِذَا أَصْبَحْتَ مُعَافًى فِي جِسْمِكَ، آمِناً فِي سَرْبِكَ، عِنْدَكَ قُوتُ يَوْمِكَ، فَعَلَى الدُّنْيَا العَفَاءُ». ١

---

١ قال السخاوي بعد تضعيفه: «لكن لهذا الحديث شواهد».

10. Asking Claimants to Support their Claims

Ali ibn al-Fadl ibn Muhammad ibn Aqil apprised us that Muhammad ibn Ab-dullah ibn Sulayman al-Hadrami apprised us that Muhammad ibn al-Ala told us that Zayd told us that Ibn Lahi'a told us that Khalid ibn Yazid al-Saksaki told us, on the authority of Sa'id ibn Abu Hilal, on the authority of Muham-mad ibn Abu al-Jahm, on the authority of al-Harith ibn Malik ﷺ, that:

He passed by the Messenger of Allah ﷺ and he asked him, "How are you this morning, O Haritha?" He said, "I woke up truly a believer." He said, "Be careful of what you say. Every truth has a reality, so what is the reality of your belief?" He said, "I have become averse to this world. It is if I am witnessing the inhabitants of Paradise visiting one another, and it is as if I am witnessing the inhabitants of the Fire bewailing one another." He said, "O Haritha, you have known, so adhere." He said it three times.

١٠. بَابٌ فِي طَلَبِ الْمُدَّعِينَ بِصِحَّةِ دَعْوَاهُمْ

أخبرنا علي بن الفضل بن محمد بن عقيل: حدثنا محمد بن عبد الله بن سليمان الحضرمي: حدثنا محمد ابن العلاء: حدثنا زيد: حدثنا ابن لَهيعة: حدثنا خالد بن يزيد السَّكْسَكي، عن سعيد بن أبي هلال، عن محمد بن أبي الجَهم، عن الحارث بن مالك ﷺ:

أَنَّهُ مَرَّ بِرَسُولِ اللهِ ﷺ فَقَالَ لَهُ: «كَيْفَ أَصْبَحْتَ يَا حَارِثَةُ»؟ فَقَالَ: أَصْبَحْتُ مُؤْمِناً حَقّاً، فَقَالَ: «انْظُرْ مَا تَقُولُ، إِنَّ لِكُلِّ حَقٍّ حَقِيقَةً، فَمَا حَقِيقَةُ إِيمَانِكَ»؟ قَالَ: عَزَفَتْ نَفْسِي عَنِ الدُّنْيَا، وَكَأَنِّي أَنْظُرُ إِلَى أَهْلِ الْجَنَّةِ يَتَزَاوَرُونَ، وَكَأَنِّي أَنْظُرُ إِلَى أَهْلِ النَّارِ يَتَضَاغَوْنَ، فَقَالَ: «يَا حَارِثَةُ، عَرَفْتَ، فَالْزَمْ». - قَالَهَا ثَلَاثاً.

27

11. Striving to Make One's Innermost Secret Match One's Outward Appearance

Abu Amr Muhammad ibn Muhammad ibn Ahmad al-Razi apprised us that Ali ibn Sa'id al-Askari told us that Abbad ibn al-Walid told us that Abu Shayban Kathir ibn Shayban told us that al-Rabi' ibn Badr told us, on the authority of Rashid ibn Muhammad, who said that Ibn Umar ﷺ said:

The Messenger of Allah ﷺ said, "The most severely punished person on the Day of Resurrection is one in whom people see good while there is no good in him."

١١. بَابُ المُجَاهَدَةِ فِي اسْتِوَاءِ السِّرِّ مَعَ الظَّاهِرِ

أخبرنا أبو عمرو محمد بن محمد بن أحمد الرازي: حدثنا علي بن سعيد العسكري: حدثنا عَبّاد بن الوليد: حدثنا أبو شيبان كثير بن شيبان: حدثنا الربيع بن بدر، عن راشد بن محمد قال: قال ابن عمر ﷺ:

قَالَ رَسُولُ اللهِ ﷺ: «أَشَدُّ النَّاسِ عَذاباً يَومَ القِيَامَةِ مَنْ يَرَى النَّاسُ فِيهِ خَيراً وَلَا خَيرَ فِيهِ».

29

12. Persistence in Remembrance of Allah, Gratitude, and Patience

Abu Amr Muhammad ibn Jaafar ibn Matar apprised us that Adam ibn Musa al-Walahanji told us that Mahmoud ibn Ghaylan told us that al-Mu'ammal told us that Hammad ibn Salama told us, on the authority of Talq ibn Habib, on the authority of Ibn Abbas 🕮, who said:

The Messenger of Allah 🕮 said, "Four matters are such that whoever is given them is given the good of this world and the hereafter: a grateful heart, a tongue busy with remembrance [of Allah], a body patient with trial, and faith in that which Allah has guaranteed."[1]

---

1 Abu Na'im narrates in *Hilyat al-Awliya* and in his collection of 40 hadith on Sufism with a different fourth item from this narration. Al-Sakhawi said, "It is good."

١٢. بابُ المُوَاظَبَةِ عَلَى الذِّكْرِ وَالشُّكْرِ وَالصَّبْرِ

أخبرنـا أبـو عمـرو محمـد بـن جعفـر بـن مطـر: حدثنـا آدم بـن موسـى الولاهنجي: حدثنا محمود بن غيلان: حدثنا المؤمل: حدثنا حماد بن سلمة، عـن طلـق بـن حبيـب، عـن ابـن عبـاس ﷺ، قـال:

قَـالَ رَسُـولُ اللهِ ﷺ: «أَرْبَـعٌ مَـنْ أُعْطِيَهُـنَّ فَقَـدْ أُعْطِـيَ خَـيْرَ الدُّنْيَا وَالْآخِرَةِ: قَلْبـاً شَـاكِراً، وَلِسَـاناً ذَاكِـراً، وَنَفْسـاً عَـلَى الْبَـلَاءِ صَابِـراً، وَثِقَـةً بِـمَا تَكَفَّـلَ اللهُ». ١

---

١   ورواه أبو نعيم في الحلية والأربعين في التصوف مع خلف في الرابع. قال السخاوي: «وهو حسن».

13. The Path of Those Devoted to Allah Most High

Abu al-Hasan Muhammad ibn Abu al-Hasan ibn Mansour apprised us that Ishaq ibn Abu Hassan al-Anmati told us that Muhammad ibn Ali ibn al-Hasan ibn Shaqiq told us that Ibrahim ibn al-Ash'ath told us that Fudayl ibn Iyad told us, on the authority of Hisham, on the authority of al-Hasan, on the authority of Imran ibn Husoyn ﷺ, who said:

The Messenger of Allah ﷺ said, "Whoever devotes himself to Allah, Allah spares him every burden and provides for him from whence he did not suspect; but whoever devotes himself to this world, Allah ﷻ consigns him to it."

١٣. بَابٌ فِي سَبِيلِ الْمُنْقَطِعِينَ إِلَى اللهِ تَعَالَى

أخبرنا أبو الحسن محمد بن أبي الحسن بن منصور: حدثنا إسحاق ابن أبي حسان الأنماطي: حدثنا محمد بن علي بن الحسن بن شقيق: حدثنا إبراهيم ابن الأشعث: حدثنا فضيل بن عياض، عن هشام، عن الحسن، عن عمران بن حصين ﷺ، قال:

قَالَ رَسُولُ اللهِ ﷺ: «مَنِ انْقَطَعَ إِلَى اللهِ كَفَاهُ اللهُ كُلَّ مُؤْنَةٍ، وَرَزَقَهُ مِنْ حَيْثُ لَا يَحْتَسِبُ، وَمَنِ انْقَطَعَ إِلَى الدُّنْيَا وَكَلَهُ اللهُ ﷻ إِلَيْهَا».

14. Their Abandonment of this World and Turning Away from It

Ali ibn Abd al-Hamid al-Ghada'iri apprised us that Abdullah ibn Mu'awiya al-Jumahi told us that Thabit ibn Yazid told us, on the authority of Hilal ibn Khabbab, on the authority of Ikrima, on the authority of Ibn Abbas ﷺ that:

Umar ibn al-Khattab ﷺ entered upon the Messenger of Allah ﷺ while he was on a straw mat that had marked up his side. [Umar] said, "O Messenger of Allah, if you would only make use of a finer sheet?" He [i.e. the Messenger] said, "What has this world to do with me?"—or "What do I have to do with this world?"—"My likeness in this world is but like a rider who traveled during a hot day until he reached a tree, and, having taken shade under it for a period of time, departed and abandoned it."[1]

---

1 It was also narrated by: Bukhari, Muslim, Tirmidhi, Ibn Hibban in his *Sahih* and al-Hakim in *al-Mustadrak*.

١٤. بَابٌ فِي تَرْكِهِمُ الدُّنْيَا وَإِعْرَاضِهِمْ عَنْهَا

أخبرنا علي بن عبد الحميد الغضائري: حدثنا عبد الله بن معاوية الجمحي: حدثنا ثابت بن يزيد، عن هلال بن خباب، عن عكرمة، عن ابن عباس ﵄:

أَنَّ عُمَرَ بْنَ الْخَطَّابِ ﵁ دَخَلَ عَلَى رَسُولِ اللهِ ﷺ وَهُوَ عَلَى حَصِيرٍ قَدْ أَثَّرَ فِي جَنْبِهِ، فَقَالَ: يَا رَسُولَ اللهِ، لَوِ اتَّخَذْتَ فِرَاشاً أَلْيَنَ مِنْ هَذَا؟ فَقَالَ: «مَا لِي وَلِلدُّنْيَا - أَوْ مَا لِلدُّنْيَا وَلِي - إِنَّمَا مَثَلِي وَمَثَلُ الدُّنْيَا كَرَاكِبٍ سَارَ فِي يَوْمٍ صَائِفٍ حَتَّى أَتَى شَجَرَةً، فَاسْتَظَلَّ فِي ظِلِّهَا سَاعَةً، ثُمَّ رَاحَ وَتَرَكَهَا».١

---

١   وأخرجه البخاري ومسلم والترمذي وابن حبّان في صحيحه والحاكم في المستدرك.

15. Love of the Needy and Neediness and The Messenger of Allah's ﷺ Wishing for it

Al-Husayn ibn Ali al-Tamimi apprised us that Abu Quraysh Muhammad ibn Jumu'a told us that Abu Sa'id al-Ashajj told us that Abu Khalid al-Ahmar told us, on the authority of Yazid ibn Sinan, on the authority of Ibn al-Mubarak, on the authority of Ata ibn Abu Rabah, on the authority of Abu Sa'id al-Khudri ﷺ who said:

I love the needy, for I truly heard the Messenger of Allah ﷺ say: "O Allah, endow me with life in neediness, cause me to die in neediness, and gather me[1] among the crowds of the needy."[2]

---

1 i.e. On Judgment Day.
2 It was also narrated by al-Hakim in *al-Mustadrak* who said, "It has an authentic chain of narrators but they did not narrate it."

١٥. بَابٌ فِي حُبِّ الْفُقَرَاءِ وَالْفَقْرِ وَسُؤَالِ رَسُولِ اللهِ ﷺ إِيَّاهُ

أخبرنا الحسين بن علي التميمي: حدثنا أبو قريش محمد بن جمعة: حدثنا أبو سعيد الأشج: حدثنا أبو خالد الأحمر، عن يزيد بن سنان، عن ابن المبارك، عن عطاء بن أبي رباح، عن أبي سعيد الخدري ﷺ، قال:

أَحِبَّ الْـمَسَاكِينَ فَإِنِّي سَمِعْتُ رَسُولَ اللهِ ﷺ يَقُولُ: «اللَّهُـمَّ أَحْيِنِي مِسْـكِيناً، وَأَمِتْنِي مِسْكِيناً، وَاحْشُرْنِي فِي زُمْرَةِ الْمَسَاكِينِ».١

---

١   ورواه الحاكم في المستدرك، وقال: «صحيح الإسناد ولم يخرجاه».

16. Their Leaving Alone that which Does not Concern Them

Abu al-Husayn al-Attar al-Hafidh apprised us in Baghdad that Muhammad ibn Muhammad ibn Sulayman told us that Ziyad ibn Barawayh al-Qas-ri told us that Yahya ibn al-Mutawakkil al-Basri told us that Yayha ibn Abu Unaysa told us, on the authority of al-Zuhri, on the authority of Ali ibn al-Husayn, on the authority of al-Harith ibn Hisham, on the authority of Ali ibn Abu Talib ﷺ who said:

The Messenger of Allah ﷺ said, "Part of one's being a good Muslim is leaving that which does not concern him."[1]

---

1 This chain of narrators is weak but other established narrations exist for this wording. Al-Sakhawi said, "This is one of four hadiths around which Islam revolves, as Abu Dawud al-Sijistani mentioned."

١٦. بَابٌ فِي تَرْكِ مَا لَا يَعْنِيهِمْ مِنَ الْأُمُورِ

أخبرنـا أبـو الحسـين العطـار الحافـظ ببغـداد: حدثنـا محمـد بـن محمـد بـن سليـمان: حدثنا زيـاد بن بارويـه القصري: حدثنا يحيـى بـن المتوكل البصري: حدثنـا يحيـى بـن أبي أنيسة، عن الزهري، عن علي بن الحسين، عن الحـارث ابـن هشـام، عـن عـلي بـن أبي طالـب ﷺ قـال:

قَـالَ رَسُـولُ اللهِ ﷺ: «مِـنْ حُسْـنِ إِسْلَامِ الْـمَرْءِ تَرْكُـهُ مَـا لَا يَعْنِيـهِ».١

---

١   هـذا الإسناد ضعيـف لكـن للمتـن روايـات أخـرى ثابتـة. قـال السخـاوي: «فهـو أحـد الأحاديـث الأربعـة التـي عليهـا مـدار الإسلام، كـما قالـه أبـو داود السجستاني».

17. Concealing their Misfortunes

Abu Ali Hamid ibn Muhammad ar-Rafa apprised us that Muhammad ibn Salih told us that Abdullah ibn Abd al-Aziz told us that my father told me, on the authority of Nafi', on the authority of Ibn Umar ☙ who said:

The Messenger of Allah ﷺ said, "Truly, concealing misfortunes is one of the treasures of piety."[1]

---

1 After mentioning various narrations for this hadith, al-Sakhawi says, "They are mutually corroborative."

١٧. بَابٌ في كِتْمَانِهِمُ الْمَصَائِبَ

أخبرنا أبو علي حامد بن محمد الرفاء: حدثنا محمد بن صالح: حدثنا عبد الله بن عبد العزيز: حدثني أبي، عن نافع، عن ابن عمر ﵄ قال:

قَالَ رَسُولُ اللهِ ﷺ: «إِنَّ مِنْ كُنُوزِ الْبِرِّ كِتْمَانَ الْمَصَائِبِ».[١]

---

١   قال السخاوي بعد ذكر طرق هذا الحديث: «وبعضها يؤكد بعضا».

18. The States of Uprightness

Muhammad ibn Abdullah ibn Ibrahim ibn Abla apprised us that Ibrahim ibn Ali told us that Yayha ibn Yahya told us that Abd al-Rahman ibn Abu al-Zinad, on the authority of his father, on the authority of Urwa ﷺ who said:

Sufyan ibn Abdullah al-Thaqafi said to the Prophet ﷺ, "Tell me something of Islam that I cannot ask of anyone else." He said, "Say, 'I believe in Allah', then remain upright."[1]

---

1   It was also narrated by Muslim and al-Nasa'i.

١٨. بَابٌ فِي أَحْوَالِ الِاسْتِقَامَةِ

أخبرنا محمـد بـن عبد الله بـن إبراهيـم بـن عبلـة: حدثنا إبراهيـم بـن علـي: حدثنا يحيى بـن يحيى: أخبرنا عبد الرحمـن بـن أبي الزنـاد، عـن أبيـه، عـن عروة ﷺ قـال:

قَـالَ سُفْيَانُ بْـنُ عَبْـدِ الله الثَّقَفِيُّ لِلنَّبِيِّ ﷺ: قُـلْ لِي فِي الْإِسْلَامِ قَوْلاً لَا أَسْأَلُ أَحَداً بَعْدَكَ. قَـالَ: «قُـلْ: آمَنْتُ بِاللهِ، ثُـمَّ اسْتَقِمْ».١

---

١   ورواه مسلم والنسائي.

19. Wearing Common Clothing

Muhammad ibn Ahmad ibn Hamdan, Abu Bakr Muhammad ibn Abdullah ibn Quraysh, and a group apprised us saying that al-Hasan ibn Sufyan apprised us that Ibn Abu al-Hawari told us that Abu al-Faqir Abd al-Aziz ibn Umayr (a resident of Damascus originally from Khorasan) told us that Zayd ibn Abu al-Zarqa told us that Jaafar ibn Burqan told us, on the authority of Maymun ibn Mahran, on the authority of Yazid ibn al-Asamm, on the authority of Umar ؓ, who said:

The Prophet ﷺ looked at Mus'ab ibn Umayr as he approached while wearing rawhide from a ram wrapped around his waist. The Prophet ﷺ said, "Look at the one in whose heart Allah has settled[1]. I saw him with parents who fed him the finest food and drink, and I truly saw him wearing an outfit that he bought—or that was bought—for 200 dirhams, but the love of Allah and the love of His Messenger led him to what you see."[2]

---

1   In another narration, it states, "Look at the one whose heart has been illumined by Allah."
2   Al-Sakhawi said, "It's narrators are well-known." He then mentioned corroborating narrations.

١٩. بَابٌ فِي لُبْسِ الْبَذْلَةِ مِنَ الثِّيَابِ

أخبرنا محمد بن أحمد بن حمدان وأبو بكر محمد بن عبد الله بن قريش وجماعة، قالوا: أخبرنا الحسن بن سفيان: حدثنا ابن أبي الحواري: حدثنا أبو الفقير عبد العزيز بن عمير من أهل خراسان نزيل دمشق: حدثنا زيد ابن أبي الزرقاء: حدثنا جعفر بن برقان، عن ميمون بن مهران، عن يزيد ابن الأصم، عن عمر ﷺ قال:

نَظَرَ النَّبِيُّ ﷺ إِلَى مُصْعَبِ بْنِ عُمَيْرٍ مُقْبِلاً، عَلَيْهِ إِهَابُ كَبْشٍ قَدْ تَنَطَّقَ بِهِ، فَقَالَ النَّبِيُّ ﷺ: «انْظُرُوا إِلَى هَذَا الَّذِي نَزَلَ¹ اللهُ قَلْبَهُ، رَأَيْتُهُ بَيْنَ أَبَوَيْنِ يَغْذُوَانِهِ بِأَطْيَبِ الطَّعَامِ وَالشَّرَابِ، وَلَقَدْ رَأَيْتُ عَلَيْهِ حُلَّةً اشْتَرَاهَا – أَوْ شُرِيَتْ – بِمِائَتَيْ دِرْهَمٍ، فَدَعَاهُ حُبُّ اللهِ وَحُبُّ رَسُولِهِ إِلَى مَا تَرَوْنَ».²

---

١   وفي بعض الروايات: «نَوَّرَ اللهُ قَلْبَهُ».
٢   قال السخاوي: «ورجاله معروفون»، ثم ذكر له شواهد.

20. Proof that Allah has Saints and *Abdal*[1] on Earth

Muhammad ibn Jaafar ibn Matar told us that Ahmad ibn Isa ibn Haroun told us that Amr ibn Yahya told us that al-Ala ibn Zaydal told us, on the authority of Anas ﷺ:

On the authority of the Prophet ﷺ, who said, "The *Abdal* of my nation are 40 men: 22 in the region of Greater Syria and 18 in Iraq. Whenever one of them dies, Allah substitutes another in his place. When the matter [of Judgment Day] arrives, they [i.e. their souls] will be collected."[2]

---

1 The *Abdal* (literally, "substitutes") are a group of 40 saints. Every time one of them passes away, he is replaced with another.
2 Al-Sakhawi notes, "Ibn al-Jawzi mentions it in his collection of fabrications." He then mentions Ibn Hibban's statement about al-Ala (the narrator), "He narrated a fabricated version on the authority of Anas. It is not permissible to mention it other than out of astonishment."

٢٠. بَابُ الدَّلِيلِ عَلَى أَنَّ للهِ فِي الْأَرْضِ أَوْلِيَاءَ وَبُدَلَاءَ

حدثنا محمد بن جعفر بن مطر: حدثنا أحمد بن عيسى بن هارون: حدثنا عمرو بن يحيى: حدثنا العلاء بن زيدل، عن أنس ﷺ:

عَنِ النَّبِيِّ ﷺ قَالَ: «بُدَلَاءُ أُمَّتِي أَرْبَعُونَ رَجُلاً، اثْنَانِ وَعِشْرُونَ بِالشَّامِ، وَثَمَانِيَةَ عَشَرَ بِالْعِرَاقِ، كُلَّمَا مَاتَ مِنْهُمْ وَاحِدٌ أَبْدَلَ اللهُ مَكَانَهُ آخَرَ، إِذَا جَاءَ الْأَمْرُ قُبِضُوا». ١.

---

١   قال السخاوي: «وقد أورده ابن الجوزي في (الموضوعات)»، ثم نقل كلام ابن حبان عن العلاء: «روى عن أنس نسخة موضوعة، لا يحل ذكره إلا تعجبا».

21. Constant Generosity in Feeding and Presenting a Table Spread

Muhammad ibn Ahmad ibn Hamdan apprised us that al-Hasan ibn Sufyan told us that Ibrahim ibn Sa'id told us that Abu Nu'aym told us that Mindal told us, on the authority of Abdullah ibn Yasar (the freeman of Aisha bin Talha), on the authority of Aisha, the Mother of Believers 🙏 who said:

The Messenger of Allah ﷺ said, "The angels remain praying for one of you as long as his table is spread out."[1]

---

1   i.e. To feed others.

٢١. بَابٌ فِي السَّخَاءِ بِالطَّعَامِ وَوَضْعِ الْمَائِدَةِ دَائِماً

أخبرنا محمد بن أحمد بن حمدان: حدثنا الحسن بن سفيان: حدثنا إبراهيم بن سعيد: حدثنا أبو نعيم: حدثنا مندل، عن عبد الله بن يسار مولى عائشة بنت طلحة، عن عائشة أم المؤمنين ﷺ قالت:

قَالَ رَسُولُ اللهِ ﷺ: «لَا تَزَالُ الْمَلَائِكَةُ تُصَلِّي عَلَى أَحَدِكُمْ مَا دَامَتْ مَائِدَتُهُ مَوْضُوعَةً».

22. Proof that the Upper Hand is that Which is Restrained from Begging

Muhammad ibn Muhammad ibn Ahmad ibn Ishaq al-Hafidh apprised us that Salih ibn Muhammad ibn Younus told us that al-Husayn ibn Abd al-Rahman al-Khorasani told us that Muhammad ibn Yousuf told us that Musa ibn Tariq told us, on the authority of Musa ibn Uqba, on the authority of Abdullah ibn Dinar, on the authority of Ibn Umar ﷺ who said:

The Messenger of Allah ﷺ said, "The upper hand is the one that is restrained and the lower hand is the one that begs."

٢٢. بَابُ الدَّلِيلِ عَلَى أَنَّ الْيَدَ الْعُلْيَا هِيَ الْمُتَعَفِّفَةُ عَنِ السُّؤَالِ

أخبرنا محمد بن محمد بن أحمد بن إسحاق الحافظ: حدثنا صالح بن محمد بن يونس: حدثنا الحسين بن عبد الرحمن الخراساني: حدثنا محمد ابن يوسف: حدثنا موسى بن طارق، عن موسى بن عقبة، عن عبد الله ابن دينار، عن ابن عمر ﷺ قال:

قَالَ رَسُولُ الله ﷺ: «الْيَدُ الْعُلْيَا الْمُتَعَفِّفَةُ، وَالْيَدُ السُّفْلَى السَّائِلَةُ».

23. Those Who Worshipped Allah in Secret and Were Rewarded for Such

Muhammad ibn Jaafar ibn Matar apprised us that Humayd ibn Ali al-Qaysi (known as "Zawj Ghanaj") told us that Hudba ibn Khalid told us that Hammad ibn Salama told us, on the authority of Thabit, on the authority of Anas ﷺ, who said:

The Messenger of Allah ﷺ said, "On the Day of Resurrection, Allah will send forth a people dressed in green garments with green wings who will descend upon the walls of Paradise. The keepers of Paradise will ask them, 'Who are you? Did you not witness [the trial of] accountability? Did you not witness the standing before Allah?' They will say, 'No, we are a people who worshipped Allah privately, and He wanted to admit us into Paradise privately.'"[1]

---

1   Al-Sakhawi quotes al-Hakim's statement regarding Zawj Ghanaj (the narrator) saying, "He is an evil liar." Ibn Hibban says about him, "We realized—assuming it was unintentional—that he had no idea what he was saying."

٢٣. بَابٌ فِيمَنْ عَبَدَ اللهَ سِرًّا فَكَافَأَهُ عَلَى ذَلِكَ

أخبرنا محمد بن جعفر بن مطر: حدثنا حميد بن علي القيسي المعروف بزوج غنج: حدثنا هدبة بن خالد: حدثنا حماد بن سلمة، عن ثابت، عن أنس ﷺ قال:

قَالَ رَسُولُ اللهِ ﷺ: «إِذَا كَانَ يَوْمُ الْقِيَامَةِ، بَعَثَ اللهُ قَوْماً عَلَيْهِمْ ثِيَابٌ خُضْرٌ بِأَجْنِحَةٍ خُضْرٍ، فَيَسْقُطُونَ عَلَى حِيطَانِ الْجَنَّةِ، فَتُشْرِفُ عَلَيْهِمْ خَزَنَةُ الْجَنَّةِ، فَيَقُولُونَ لَهُمْ: مَنْ أَنْتُمْ؟ أَمَا شَهِدْتُمُ الْحِسَابَ؟ وَمَا شَهِدْتُمُ الْوُقُوفَ بَيْنَ يَدَيِ اللهِ؟ فَقَالُوا: لَا، نَحْنُ قَوْمٌ عَبَدْنَا اللهَ سِرًّا، فَأَحَبَّ أَنْ يُدْخِلَنَا الْجَنَّةَ سِرًّا». [١]

---

[١] نقل السخاوي كلام الحاكم في زوج غنج، فقال: «إنه كذاب خبيث»، وكلام ابن حبان: «وعلمنا أنه إن لم يتعمد، فإنه لا يدري ما يقول».

24. Contentment, Scrupulousness, Compassion Towards Muslims, Being a Good Companion, and Laughing Little

Muhammad ibn Zayd ibn Muhammad apprised us that Ahmad ibn al-Abbas ibn Hazm told us that Muhammad ibn Isma'il told us that al-Muharibi told us, on the authority of Abu Raja al-Khorasani, on the authority of Burd ibn Sinan, on the authority of Makhool, on the authority of Wathila ibn al-Asqa', on the authority of Abu Hurayra ﷺ who said:

The Messenger of Allah ﷺ told me: "O Abu Hurayra, be scrupulous and you will be the most devoted of people; be content and you will be the most grateful of people; love for people what you love for yourself and you will be a believer; be a good companion to those in your company and you will be a Muslim; and decrease laughter, for truly, a lot of laughter kills the heart."[1]

---

1   Ibn Majah related it with a good chain of narrators.

٢٤. بَابٌ فِي الْقَنَاعَةِ وَالْوَرَعِ وَالشَّفَقَةِ عَلَى الْمُسْلِمِينَ وَحُسْنِ الْمُجَاوَرَةِ وَقِلَّةِ الضَّحِكِ

أَخبَرَنا مُحمَّد بن زيد بن محمد: حدثنا أحمد بن العباس بن حزم: حدثنا محمد بن إسماعيل: حدثنا المحاربي، عن أبي رجاء الخراساني، عن برد بن سنان، عن مكحول، عن واثلة بن الأسقع، عن أبي هريرة ﵁، قال:

قَالَ لِي رَسُولُ اللهِ ﷺ: «يَا أَبَا هُرَيْرَةَ، كُنْ وَرِعاً تَكُنْ أَعْبَدَ النَّاسِ، وَكُنْ قَنِعاً تَكُنْ أَشْكَرَ النَّاسِ، وَأَحِبَّ لِلنَّاسِ مَا تُحِبُّ لِنَفْسِكَ تَكُنْ مُؤْمِناً، وَأَحْسِنْ مُجَاوَرَةَ مَنْ جَاوَرَكَ تَكُنْ مُسْلِماً، وَأَقِلَّ الضَّحِكَ فَإِنَّ كَثْرَةَ الضَّحِكِ تُمِيتُ الْقَلْبَ».١

---

١ أخرجه ابن ماجه بإسناد حسن.

25. Choosing Poverty over Affluence

Sulayman ibn Muhammad ibn Najiya al-Madini apprised us that Abu Amr Ahmad ibn al-Mubarak al-Mustamili told us that Abu Khalid al-Farra told us that Abdullah ibn al-Mubarak told us, on the authority of Yahya ibn Ayyub, on the authority of Abaydullah ibn Zahr, on the authority of Ali ibn Yazid, on the authority of al-Qasim, on the authority of Abu Umama ﷺ who said:

The Messenger of Allah ﷺ said, "My lord offered to turn the riverbed of Mecca into gold for me, so I said, 'No, my lord! Rather, let me eat my fill one day and go hungry the next so that when I am hungry, I might humble myself before You, and when I am full, I might praise You and mention You in remembrance.'"

٢٥. بَابٌ في اخْتِيَارِ الْفَقْرِ عَلَى الْغِنَى

أخبرنا سليمان بن محمد بن ناجية المديني: حدثنا أبو عمرو أحمد بن المبارك المستملي: حدثنا أبو خالد الفراء: حدثنا عبد الله بن المبارك، عن يحيى بن أيوب، عن عبيد الله بن زحر، عن علي بن يزيد، عن القاسم، عن أبي أمامة ﵁ قال:

قَالَ رَسُولُ الله ﷺ: «عَرَضَ عَلَيَّ رَبِّي أَنْ يَجْعَلَ لِي بَطْحَاءَ مَكَّةَ ذَهَباً، فَقُلْتُ: لَا، يَا رَبِّ، وَلَكِنْ أَشْبَعُ يَوْماً وَأَجُوعُ يَوْماً، فَإِذَا جُعْتُ تَضَرَّعْتُ إِلَيْكَ، وَإِذَا شَبِعْتُ حَمِدْتُكَ وَذَكَرْتُكَ».

26. Supporting the Poor Before One's Family and Dependents

Muhammad ibn Nasr ibn Ashkib al-Zaafarani al-Bukhari apprised us that Hamid ibn Sahl told us that Ibn Abu Umar told us that Sufyan told us, on the authority of Ata ibn al-Sa'ib, on the authority of his father, on the authority of Ali ﷻ:

The Messenger of Allah ﷺ told Fatima, "I will not give you and leave the People of al-Suffah with their bellies wrenching in hunger."

Isma'il ibn Ahmad al-Jurjani apprised us that Muhammad ibn al-Hasan ibn Qutayba al-Askalani apprised us that Hamid ibn Yahya told us that Sufyan told us the same. [1]

---

1   It was also narrated by Imam Ahmad. Al-Sakhawi said, "Its chain of narrtors is authentic."

٢٦. بَابٌ فِي الِابْتِدَاءِ بِتَعَهُّدِ الْفُقَرَاءِ دُونَ الْأَهْلِ وَالْعِيَالِ

أخبرنـا محمـد بـن نصـر بـن أشكيب الزعفرانـي البخـاري: حدثنـا حامـد بـن سهل: حدثنا ابن أبي عمر: حدثنا سفيان، عن عطَاء بن السَّائب، عن أبيه، عـن عـلي ﵁:

أَنَّ النَّبِيَّ ﷺ قَالَ لِفَاطِمَةَ: «لَا أُعْطِيكُمْ وَأَدَعُ أَهْلَ الصُّفَّةِ تُطْوَى بُطُونُهُمْ مِنَ الْجُوعِ».

أخبرنا إسماعيل بـن أحمـد الجرجـاني: أخبرنـا محمـد بـن الحسـن بـن قتيبة العسـقلاني: حدثنا حامـد بـن يحيى: حدثنـا سفيـان بمثلـه.١

---

١   رواه الإمام أحمد، وقال السخاوي: «وسنده صحيح».

27. The Permissibility of Speaking through Singularity[1]

Muhammad ibn al-Hasan ibn Isma'il al-Siraj apprised us that Muhammad ibn Abdullah ibn Sulayman al-Hadrami Mutayyan told us that Ali ibn Mundhir told us that Ibn Fudayl told us that my father told us, on the authority of Nafi', on the authority of Ibn Umar ﷺ who said:

When the Messenger of Allah ﷺ passed away, Abu Bakr appeared and climbed the pulpit. He then praised Allah, glorified Him, and said, "If Muhammad was your god that you worship, then your god has died. However, if your god is the One in the Heavens, then your god is living and does not die." He then recited, *"Muhammad is only a messenger; messengers have passed away before him."* [2] [3]

---

1 Singularity (Ar. *tafrid*) is an intense awareness of the Oneness of Allah.
2 *Aal Imran*, 3:144.
3 Al-Bazzar also narrated it. Al-Sakhawi said, "It is authentic."

٢٧. بَابُ إِبَاحَةِ الْكَلَامِ عَلَى لِسَانِ التَّفْرِيدِ

أَخْبَرَنَا محمدُ بنُ الحسنِ بنِ إسماعيلَ السراجُ: حدثنا محمدُ بنُ عبدِ اللهِ بنِ سليمانَ الحضرميُّ مطينٌ: حدثنا عليُّ بنُ منذرٍ: حدثنا ابنُ فضيلٍ: حدثنا أبي، عن نافعٍ، عن ابنِ عمرَ ﵄ قال:

لَمَّا قُبِضَ رَسُولُ اللهِ ﷺ أَتَى أَبُو بَكْرٍ، فَصَعِدَ الْمِنْبَرَ، فَحَمِدَ اللهَ وَأَثْنَى عَلَيْهِ، وَقَالَ: إِنْ كَانَ مُحَمَّدٌ إِلَـهَكُمُ الَّذِي تَعْبُدُونَ فَإِنَّ إِلَـهَكُمْ قَدْ مَاتَ، وَإِنْ كَانَ إِلَهُكُمُ الَّذِي فِي السَّمَاوَاتِ فَإِنَّ إِلَـهَكُمْ حَيٌّ لَا يَمُوتُ، ثُمَّ تَلَا: ﴿وَمَا مُحَمَّدٌ إِلَّا رَسُولٌ قَدْ خَلَتْ مِنْ قَبْلِهِ الرُّسُلُ﴾[21].

---

١ آل عمران ٣: ١٤٤.
٢ ورواه البزار. قال السخاوي: «وهو صحيح».

28. Sheikhs Personally Serving Visitors and Strangers

Abu al-Abbas al-Asamm apprised us that Helal ibn al-Alaa al-Raqqi told us; Abdullah ibn Muhammad ibn Ali ibn Ziyad also apprised us that Muhammad ibn Hamdoun told us that Hilal ibn al-Alaa told us that my father told us that Talha ibn Zayd told us that al-Awza'i told us, on the authority of Yahya ibn Abu Kathir, on the authority of Abu Salama, on the authority of Abu Qatada, who said:

The Negus' delegation came to the Prophet ﷺ and he took up serving them. His companions told him, "We will spare you that." He said, "Truly, they were honourable to my companions, and I want to repay them."

Ahmad ibn Ali al-Muqri apprised us that Hilal told us something similar.[1]

---

1 Al-Sakhawi says, "Al-Nasa'i said, 'I witnessed false hadiths by al-Ala.' Ibn Hibban said, 'It is not permissible to cite him.' His teacher was very weak, and was even accused of fabrication."

٢٨. بَابٌ فِي خِدْمَةِ الْمَشَايِخِ بِأَنْفُسِهِمُ الْوَافِدَ عَلَيْهِمْ وَالْغَرِيبَ

أخبرنا أبو العباس الأصم: حدثنا هلال بن العلاء الرَّقِّي. وأخبرنا عبد الله بن محمد بن علي بن زياد: حدثنا محمد بن حمدون: حدثنا هلال بن العلاء: حدثنا أبي: حدثنا طلحة بن زيد: حدثنا الأوزاعي، عن يحيى بن أبي كثير، عن أبي سلمة، عن أبي قتادة، قال:

قَدِمَ وَفْدُ النَّجَاشِيِّ عَلَى النَّبِيِّ ﷺ، فَقَامَ بِخِدْمَتِهِمْ، فَقَالَ لَهُ أَصْحَابُهُ: نَحْنُ نَكْفِيكَ ذَلِكَ، قَالَ: «إِنَّهُمْ كَانُوا لِأَصْحَابِي مُكْرِمِينَ، وَأَنَا أُحِبُّ أَنْ أُكَافِئَهُمْ».

وأخبرنا أحمد بن علي المقرئ: حدثنا هلال بنحوه.[1]

---

١ قال السخاوي: «و قد قال النسائي: رأيت للعلاء أحاديث مناكير، وقال ابن حبان: لا يجوز الاحتجاج به. وشيخه صعيف جدا، بل اتهم بالوضع».

29. Adopting Patched Clothing and Wearing It

Ali ibn Bundar ibn al-Husayn al-Sufi apprised us that Muhammad ibn Ali ibn Sa'id al-Markab told us that Muhammad ibn Abdullah al-Mukharrimi told us that Muhammad ibn Hafs told us that Warqa told us, on the authority of Abu Ishaq, on the authority of Yahya, on the authority of Umm al-Husoyn, who said:

I was in Aisha's 🕮 residence while she was patching a tunic of hers with variously-coloured patches: some white, some black, and some other than that. The Prophet 🕮 entered and said, "What is this, O Aisha?" She said, "A tunic of mine that I am patching." He said, "Well done. Do not abandon a garment until you have patched it, for there is nothing new to someone who does not have anything shabby."[1]

---

1   Al-Sakhawi said, "Its narrators are reliable."

٢٩. بَابٌ فِي اتِّخَاذِ الْمُرَقَّعَةِ وَلُبْسِهَا

أخبرنا علي بن بندار بن الحسين الصوفي: حدثنا محمد بن علي بن سعيد المركب: حدثنا محمد بن عبد الله المخرمي: حدثنا محمد بن حفص: حدثنا ورقاء، عن أبي إسحاق، عن يحيى، عن أم الحصين، قالت:

كُنْتُ فِي بَيْتِ عَائِشَةَ ﵂ وَهِيَ تُرَقِّعُ قَمِيصاً لَهَا بِأَلْوَانٍ مِنْ رِقَاعٍ، بَعْضُهَا بَيَاضٌ، وَبَعْضُهَا سَوَادٌ، وَبَعْضُهَا غَيْرُ ذَلِكَ، فَدَخَلَ النَّبِيُّ ﷺ فَقَالَ: «مَا هَذَا يَا عَائِشَةُ»؟ قَالَتْ: قَمِيصٌ لِي أُرَقِّعُهَا. فَقَالَ: «أَحْسَنْتِ، لَا تَضَعِي ثَوْباً حَتَّى تُرَقِّعِيهِ، فَإِنَّهُ لَا جَدِيدَ لِمَنْ لَا خَلَقَ[1] لَهُ».[2]

---

١ ثَوْبٌ خَلَقٌ—بفتح اللام—أي بالٍ.
٢ قال السخاوي: «ورجاله ثقات».

30. Taking a Water Skin During Travels[1]

Yusuf ibn Ya'qub ibn Ibrahim al-Abhari apprised us that Muhammad ibn Abd al-Rahman ibn Asad al-Qadi told us that Asad ibn Muhammad told us, that Abu Jaber told us that Sa'id ibn Yazid told us, on the authority of Jaafar ibn Muhammad, on the authority of his father, on the authority of his grandfather, on the authority of his father, on the authority of his grandfather, who said:

The Prophet ﷺ left to a distant, open area, so I took a water skin and followed him.

He [(i.e. the narrator)] mentioned the hadith.

---

1   i.e. Taking water with one during travel in order to clean oneself after answering the call of nature.

٣٠. بَابٌ فِي أَخْذِ الرَّكْوَةِ فِي الْأَسْفَارِ

أخبرنا يوسف بن يعقوب بن إبراهيم الأبهري: حدثنا محمد بن عبد الرحمن ابن أسد القاضي: حدثنا أسد بن محمد: حدثنا أبو جابر: حدثنا سعيد بن يزيد، عن جعفر بن محمد، عن أبيه، عن جده، عن أبيه، عن جده، قال:

خَرَجَ النَّبِيُّ ﷺ [إلى]¹ الْبَرَازِ، فَأَخَذْتُ رَكْوَةً، فَخَرَجْتُ فِي إِثْرِهِ.

وذكر الحديث.

---

١ بدون لفظ «إلى» في الأصل ولعله سقط.

31. The Sunnah of Gathering over Food and the Reprehensibility of Eating Individually

Isma'il ibn Ahmad al-Jurjani apprised us that Muhammad ibn al-Hasan ibn Qutayba apprised us that Ahmad ibn abd al-Aziz al-Wasiti told us that al-Walid ibn Muslim told us that Wahshi ibn Harb ibn Wahshi told us, on the authority of his father, on the authority of his grandfather, that:

A man said, "O Messenger of Allah, truly we eat but do not feel full." He said, "Perhaps you split up when eating. Gather over it and mention the name of Allah ﷻ and you will be blessed therein."[1]

---

1 It was also narrated by Abu Dawud, and Ibn Majah, as well as al-Hakim and Ibn Hibban in their *Sahih* collections.

٣١. بَابُ السُّنَّةِ فِي الِاجْتِمَاعِ عَلَى الطَّعَامِ وَكَرَاهِيَةِ الأَكْلِ فُرَادَى

أخبرنا إسماعيل بن أحمد الجرجاني: أخبرنا محمد بن الحسن بن قتيبة: حدثنا أحمد بن عبد العزيز الواسطي: حدثنا الوليد بن مسلم: حدثنا وحشي بن حرب بن وحشي، عن أبيه، عن جده:

أَنَّ رَجُلاً قَالَ: يَا رَسُولَ الله، إِنَّا نَأْكُلُ فَلَا نَشْبَعُ، فَقَالَ: «لَعَلَّكُمْ تَفْتَرِقُونَ عَلَى طَعَامِكُمْ، اجْتَمِعُوا عَلَيْهِ، وَاذْكُرُوا اسْمَ الله ﷻ يُبَارَكْ لَكُمْ فِيهِ».[1]

_____

١   أخرجه أبو داود وابن ماجه وأحمد والحاكم وابن حبان في صحيحيهما.

32. The Permissibility of Speaking about Esoteric Knowledge and Its Reality

Hamed ibn Abdullah al-Harawi apprised us that Nasr ibn Muhammad ibn al-Harith al-Buzjani told us that Abd al-Salam ibn Saleh told us that Sufyan ibn Uyayna told us, on the authority of Ibn Jurayj, on the authority of Ata, on the authority of Abu Hurayra ؓ:

The Messenger of Allah said, "Truly, some knowledge is like a concealed form: no one knows it except for those with knowledge of Allah ﷻ and, when they speak of it, no one disapproves of it except for those heedless of Allah the Exalted."[1]

---

1 Abd al-Salam ibn Saleh is Abu al-Salt al-Harawi, who is very weak according to the majority of scholars. Al-Hakim said, "The Imam of Hadith, Yahya ibn Ma'in, attested to his worthiness."

٣٢. بَابُ إِبَاحَةِ الْكَلَامِ فِي بَاطِنِ الْعِلْمِ وَحَقِيقَتِهِ

أخبرنا حامد بن عبد الله الهروي: حدثنا نصر بن محمد بن الحارث البوزجاني: حدثنا عبد السلام بن صالح: حدثنا سفيان بن عيينة، عن ابن جريج، عن عطاء، عن أبي هريرة ﵁:

أَنَّ رَسُولَ الله ﷺ قَالَ: «إِنَّ مِنَ الْعِلْمِ كَهَيْئَةِ الْمَكْنُونِ، لَا يَعْرِفُهُ إِلَّا الْعُلَمَاءُ بِاللهِ ﷿، فَإِذَا نَطَقُوا بِهِ لَا يُنْكِرُهُ إِلَّا أَهْلُ الْغِرَّةِ بِاللهِ تَعَالَى».١

---

١ عبد السلام بن صالح هو أبو الصلت الهروي، وهو ضعيف جدا عند الجمهور. قال الحاكم: «وثّقه إمام الحديث يحيى بن معين»

33. Avoiding Extravagance with Guests and Serving them What is Available

Muhammad ibn Muhammad ibn Ya'qub al-Hafidh apprised us that Muhammad ibn Sa'id ibn Imran told us that Ahmad ibn Abdullah ibn Zeyad al-Iyadi told us that Musa ibn Muhammad al-Sukkari told us that Baqiyya ibn al-Walid said that Isma'il ibn Yahya al-Taymi told us, on the authority of Mis'ar, on the authority of Amr ibn Murra, on the authority of Abu al-Bakhtari, who said:

We visited Salman al-Farisi in al-Mada'in. He brought us bread and fish and said, "Eat. The Messenger of Allah 鑿 disallowed extravagance, and were it not for this, I would have certainly made extravagant preparations for you."[1]

---

1   Al-Hakim narrates a similar hadith in *al-Mustadrak* and said, "It has an authentic chain of narrators but they did not narrate it."

٣٣. بَابُ تَرْكِ التَّكَلُّفِ لِلضَّيْفِ وَإِحْضَارِهِ مَا حَضَرَهُ

أخبرنا محمد بن محمد بن يعقوب الحافظ: حدثنا محمد بن سعيد بن عمران: حدثنا أحمد بن عبد الله بن زياد الإيادي: حدثنا موسى بن محمد السكري: حدثنا بقية بن الوليد: حدثنا إسماعيل بن يحيى التيمي، عن مسعر، عن عمرو بن مرة، عن أبي البختري، قال:

نَزَلْنَا عَلَى سَلْمَانَ الْفَارِسِيِّ بِالْمَدَائِنِ، فَقَرَّبَ إِلَيْنَا خُبْزاً وَسَمَكاً، وَقَالَ: كُلُوا، نَهَانَا رَسُولُ الله ﷺ عَنِ التَّكَلُّفِ، وَلَوْلَا ذَلِكَ لَتَكَلَّفْتُ لَكُمْ.[1]

---

[1] روى مثله الحاكم في المستدرك، وقال: «إنه صحيح الإسناد ولم يخرجاه».

34. Avoiding Luxury

Muhammad ibn Muhammad ibn Ya'qub al-Hafidh apprised us that Sa'id ibn Abd al-Aziz told us that Ibn Musaffa told us that Baqiyya told us that al-Sari ibn Yan'um told us, on the authority of Murayh ibn Masrouq al-Hawzani, on the authority of Muadh ibn Jabal ﷺ:

When the Prophet ﷺ sent him to Yemen, he said, "Beware of luxury, for the slaves of Allah are not men of luxury."[1]

---

1   Abu Na'im narrates this in his collection of 40 hadith on Sufism, and al-Sakhawi authenticated his narrators.

٣٤. بَابٌ فِي تَرْكِ التَّنَعُّمِ

أخبرنا محمـد بـن محمـد بـن يعقوب الحافظ: حدثنا سعيد بـن عبد العزيـز: حدثنا ابن مصفى: حدثنا بقية: حدثنا السري بن ينعم، عن مريح بن مسروق الهـوزني، عن معـاذ بـن جبـل ﷺ:

أَنَّ النَّبِيَّ ﷺ لَمَّا بَعَثَهُ إِلَى الْيَمَنِ قَالَ: «إِيَّاكَ وَالتَّنَعُّمَ، فَإِنَّ عِبَادَ اللهِ لَيْسُوا بِالْمُتَنَعِّمِينَ».¹

---

١   رواه أبو نعيم في الأربعين ووثّق رواته السخاوي.

35. Received Tradition that Attests to Perspicacity

Ahmad ibn Ali al-Razi apprised us that Muhammed ibn Ahmad ibn al-Sakan told us that Musa ibn Dawud told us that Muhammad ibn Kathir al-Kufi told us that Amr ibn Qays told us, on the authority of Atiyya, on the authority of Abu Sa'id ﷺ who said:

The Messenger of Allah ﷺ said, "Be wary of the perspicacity of a believer, for truly, he sees with the light of Allah the Exalted."[1]

---

1 After mentioning various narrations for this hadith, al-Sakhawi says, "These narrations strengthen each other."

٣٥. بَابُ مَا جَاءَ فِي تَصْحِيحِ الْفِرَاسَةِ

أخبرنا أحمد بن علي الرازي: حدثنا محمد بن أحمد بن السكن: حدثنا موسى بن داود: حدثنا محمد بن كثير الكوفي: حدثنا عمرو بن قيس، عن عطية، عن أبي سعيد ﷺ قال:

قَالَ رَسُولُ اللهِ ﷺ: «اتَّقُوا فِرَاسَةَ الْمُؤْمِنِ، فَإِنَّهُ يَنْظُرُ بِنُورِ اللهِ تَعَالَى».[١]

---

١   قال السخاوي بعد ذكر طرق هذا الحديث: «وبعضها يتقوى ببعض».

36. Attaining the Love of Allah the Exalted by Constantly Serving Him

Ahmad ibn Muhammad ibn Abdous al-Tara'ifi apprised us that Uthman ibn Sa'id al-Darimi told us that Sa'id ibn Abu Maryam told us that Yahya ibn Ayoub told us that Ibn Zahr apprised us, on the authority of Ali ibn Yazid, on the authority of al-Qasim, on the authority of Abu Umama ﷺ:

The Messenger of Allah ﷺ said: "Allah ﷻ said, 'The slave continues to draw closer to me by supererogatory works until I love him. When I love him, I am his hearing with which he hears, his sight with which he sees, his tongue with which he speaks, and his heart with which he comprehends. If he then invokes Me, I will respond to him, and if he asks of Me, I will bestow upon him.'"[1]

---

1   It was also narrated by al-Bukhari.

٣٦. بَابُ اسْتِجْلَابِ مَحَبَّةِ اللهِ تَعَالَى بِالْمُدَاوَمَةِ عَلَى خِدْمَتِهِ

أخبرنا أحمد بن محمد بن عبدوس الطرائفي: حدثنا عثمان بن سعيد الدارمي: حدثنا سعيد بن أبي مريم: حدثنا يحيى بن أيوب: أخبرنا ابن زحر، عن علي بن يزيد، عن القاسم، عن أبي أمامة ﵁:

أَنَّ رَسُولَ اللهِ ﷺ قَالَ: «قَالَ اللهُ ﷻ: مَا زَالَ الْعَبْدُ يَتَقَرَّبُ إِلَيَّ بِالنَّوَافِلِ حَتَّى أُحِبَّهُ، فَإِذَا أَحْبَبْتُهُ فَأَكُونُ سَمْعَهُ الَّذِي يَسْمَعُ بِهِ، وَبَصَرَهُ الَّذِي يُبْصِرُ بِهِ، وَلِسَانَهُ الَّذِي يَنْطِقُ بِهِ، وَقَلْبَهُ الَّذِي يَعْقِلُ بِهِ، فَإِذَا دَعَانِي أَجَبْتُهُ، وَإِذَا سَأَلَنِي أَعْطَيْتُهُ». ١

---

١   ورواه البخاري.

37. The Reprehensibility of Amassing Wealth Lest the Slave Covet this World

Abu Amr ibn Matar apprised us that Abu Khalifa told us that al-Ramadi told us that Ibn Uyayna told us, on the authority of al-A'mash, on the authority of Shammar ibn Atiyya, on the authority of al-Mughira ibn Saad ibn al-Akhram, on the authority of his father, on the authority of Abdullah ﷺ who said:

The Messenger of Allah ﷺ said, "Do not become pre-occupied with earnings lest you covet this world.[1]"[2]

---

1   A more literal translation would be, "Do not acquire pastoral lands…" The Arabic word *day'ah*, while literally referring to pastoral lands and agriculture, can also refer to any means of earning a living. The upshot of the hadith is that one should not become pre-occupied with earning a living, not that one should abandon earning a living altogether if it entails begging or depending on others, both of which are ignoble for able-bodied young men.

2   It was also narrated by Ibn Hibban in his *Sahih* and al-Tirmidhi who said, "It is a good [hadith]."

٣٧. بَابُ كَرَاهِيَةِ جَمْعِ الْمَالِ لِئَلَّا يَرْغَبَ الْعَبْدُ فِي الدُّنْيَا

أخبرنـا أبـو عمـرو بـن مطـر: حدثنـا أبـو خليفـة: حدثنـا الرمـادي:
حدثنـا ابـن عيينـة، عـن الأعمـش، عـن شـمر بـن عطيـة، عـن المغيـرة بـن سـعد بـن
الأخـرم، عـن أبيـه، عـن عبـد الله ﷺ قـال:

قَـالَ رَسُـولُ اللهِ ﷺ: «لَا تَتَّخِـذُوا الضَّيْعَـةَ فَتَرْغَبُـوا فِي
الدُّنْيَـا».[١]

---

١   رواه ابن حبان في صحيحه والترمذي، وقال: «إنه حسن».

38. The Manner of Judicious People

Abdullah ibn Muhammad ibn Ali apprised us that Ali ibn Sa'id al-Askari told us that Ahmad ibn Yahya ibn Malik al-Sousi told us that Dawud ibn al-Muhabbar told us that Abbad ibn Kathir told us, on the authority of Abdullah ibn Dinar, on the authority of Abdullah ibn Umar, who said:

The Messenger of Allah ﷺ said, "The judicious person is one who understands what Allah requires of him."[1]

---

1   Al-Sakhawi says regarding Dawud, "He is rejected."

٣٨. بَابٌ فِي صِفَةِ الْعُقَلَاءِ

أخبرنا عبد الله بن محمد بن علي: حدثنا علي بن سعيد العسكري: حدثنا أحمد بن يحيى بن مالك السوسي: حدثنا داود بن المحبر: حدثنا عباد بن كثير، عن عبد الله بن دينار، عن عبد الله بن عمر، قال:

قَالَ رَسُولُ اللهِ ﷺ: «الْعَاقِلُ الَّذِي عَقَلَ عَنِ اللهِ أَمْرَهُ».¹

---

١   قال السخاوي في داود: «وهو تالف».

39. The Permissibility of Listening to Singing

Muhammad ibn Muhammad ibn Ya'qoub al-Hafidh apprised us that Muhammad ibn Abdullah ibn Yousuf al-Harawi told us in Damscus that Sa'id ibn Muhammad ibn Zurayq al-Ras'ani told us that Abd al-Aziz al-Uwaysi told us that Ibrahim ibn Saad told us, on the authority of Muhammad ibn Ishaq, on the authority of Uthman ibn Urwa, on the authority of his father:

On the authority of Aisha, who said, "The Messenger of Allah ﷺ came over during the Days of Tashriq[1] when I had two of Abdullah ibn Salam's girls with me, striking their tambourines and singing. When the Messenger of Allah ﷺ entered, I said, 'Stop.' The Messenger of Allah ﷺ withdrew to a bed, lay down on his side, and covered himself with his garment. I said, 'Today, singing will most certainly be made permissible or forbidden.'" She said, "I indicated to them to commence." She said, "So they commenced, and by Allah, I did not forget this: Abu Bakr entered—and he was a marching man (by which he[2] meant stern)—saying, 'Are the flutes of Satan in the

---

1   i.e. The three days following Eid al-Adha.
2   i.e. The narrator.

٣٩. بَابٌ فِي إِبَاحَةِ السَّمَاعِ

أخبرنـا محمـد بـن محمـد بـن يعقـوب الحافـظ: حدثنـا محمـد بـن عبـد الله بـن يوسف الهروي بدمشق: حدثنا سعيد بن محمد بن زريق الرسعني: حدثنا عبد العزيز الأويسي: حدثنا إبراهيم بـن سعد، عن محمـد بـن إسحاق، عن عثمان بن عروة، عن أبيه:

عَنْ عَائِشَةَ، قَالَتْ: دَخَـلَ رَسُـولُ الله ﷺ فِي أَيَّامِ التَّشْرِيـقِ وَعِنْدِي جَارِيَتَانِ لِعَبْدِ الله بْـنِ سَلَامٍ تَضْرِبَـانِ بِدُفَّيْنِ لَهُمَا وَتُغَنِّيَانِ، فَلَمَّا دَخَـلَ رَسُـولُ الله ﷺ قُلْتُ: أَمْسِكَا، فَتَنَحَّى رَسُـولُ الله ﷺ إِلَى سَرِيـرٍ فِي الْبَيْتِ، فَاضْطَجَعَ، وَسَجَّى بِثَوْبِهِ، فَقُلْتُ: لَيُحَلَّـنَّ الْيَـوْمَ الْغِنَـاءُ أَوْ لَيُحَرَّمَـنَّ، قَالَـتْ: فَأَشَرْتُ إِلَيْهِمَا أَنْ خُـذَا، قَالَـتْ: فَأَخَذَتَا، فَـوَالله مَا نَسِيتُ ذَلِـكَ: أَنْ دَخَـلَ أَبُـو بَكْـرٍ - وَكَانَ رَجُـلًا مَطَّـاراً - يَعْنِـي حَدِيـداً - وَهُـوَ يَقُـولُ: أَمَزَامِيـرُ الشَّيْطَانِ فِي بَيْـتِ رَسُـولِ الله ﷺ؟ فَكَشَفَ رَسُـولُ الله ﷺ رَأْسَـهُ، وَقَـالَ: «يَـا أَبَـا بَكْـرٍ، لِكُـلِّ قَـوْمٍ عِيـدٌ، وَهَـذَا أَيَّـامُ عِيدِنَـا».[١]

---

[١] قال السخاوي: «وأصل الحديث في الصحيحين».

85

house of the Messenger of Allah ﷺ?' The Messenger
of Allah ﷺ then uncovered his head and said, 'O Abu
Bakr, every people have a holiday, and this is during
the days of our holiday.'"[1]

---

1   Al-Sakhawi said, "Similar narrations exist in the two Sahih collections."

40. The Permissibility of Dancing

Abu al-Abbas Ahmad ibn Sa'id al-Maadani apprised us in Merv that Muhammad ibn Sa'id al-Mirwazi told us that al-Tuqufi told us that Abdullah ibn Amr al-Warraq told us that al-Hasan ibn Ali ibn Mansour told us that Ghiyath al-Basri told us, on the authority of Ibrahim ibn Muhammad al-Shafi'i:

Sa'id ibn al-Musayyib passed through some of the alleys of Mecca when he heard al-Akhdar al-Jaddi singing in the home of al-As ibn Wael:

Sweet musk poured forth from deep within Na'man[1]
When, with perfumed dames, Zaynab walked its streets.
But when she saw Numayri's caravan,
She dodged him, as the ladies feared they'd meet!

He[2] said, "He[3] tapped his foot against the ground for a period of time and said, 'It is this that delights the hearing.' They opined that the poetry was by Sa'id."[4]

---

1 Na'man is the proper name of a place in the Hijaz region of Western Arabia.
2 i.e. The narrator.
3 i.e. Sa'id ibn al-Musayyib.
4 Another hadith related to the permissibility of dancing is that which Muslim narrated regarding the Abyssinians.

٤٠. بَابٌ فِي إِبَاحَةِ الرَّقْصِ

أخبرنا أبو العباس أحمد بن سعيد المعداني الفقيه بمرو: حدثنا محمد بن سعيد المروزي: حدثنا الترقفي، حدثنا عبد الله بن عمرو الوراق، حدثنا الحسن بن علي بن منصور، حدثنا غياث البصري، عن إبراهيم بن محمد الشافعي:

أَنَّ سَعِيدَ بْنَ الْمُسَيِّبِ مَرَّ فِي بَعْضِ أَزِقَّةِ مَكَّةَ، فَسَمِعَ الْأَخْضَرَ الْجَدِّيَّ يَتَغَنَّى فِي دَارِ الْعَاصِ بْنِ وَائِلٍ:

بِهِ زَيْنَبٌ فِي نِسْوَةٍ عَطِرَاتِ	تَضَوَّعَ مِسْكاً بَطْنُ نَعْمَانَ أَنْ مَشَتْ
وَكُنَّ مِنْ أَنْ يَلْقَيْنَهُ حَذِرَاتِ	فَلَمَّا رَأَتْ رَكْبَ النُّمَيْرِيِّ أَعْرَضَتْ

قَالَ: فَضَرَبَ بِرِجْلِهِ الْأَرْضَ زَمَاناً، وَقَالَ: هَذَا مَا يَلَذُّ سَمَاعُهُ، وَكَانَ يَرَوْنَ أَنَّ الشِّعْرَ لِسَعِيدٍ.[1]

---

١   ومما ذكر في هذا الباب حديث الأحباش الذي رواه مسلم.

89

This book is complete. Praise is due to Allah, a praise that He rightfully deserves. May His blessings be upon the Best of His Creation, his family, and companions; and may He whelm multitudinous greetings of peace upon them. And Allah is sufficient for us; an excellent Guardian is He!

تــم الكتــاب، والحمــد لله حــق حمـده، وصلواتـه عـلى خيرتـه مـن خلقـه وآلـه وصحبـه وسـلم تسـليما كثـيرا، وحسـبنا الله ونعـم الوكيـل.

OTHER BOOKS PUBLISHED BY MABDA

Islam Series

1. *The Amman Message* 2008
2. *Forty Hadith on Divine Mercy* 2009
3. *Jihad and the Islamic Law of War* 2009
4. *The Holy Qur'an and the Environment* 2010
5. *Islam and Peace* 2012
6. *Reason and Rationality in the Qur'an* 2012
7. *The Concept of Faith in Islam* 2012
8. *Warfare in the Qur'an* 2012
9. *Condemning Terrorism* 2012
10. *The Qur'an and Combat by* **Imam Mahmoud Muhammad Shaltut** 2012
11. *What is Islam, and Why?* 2012
12. *How to Integrate the Remembrance of God into Teaching* 2012
13. *On Invoking the Divine Name 'Allah'* 2012
14. *True Islam* 2006
15. *War and Peace in Islam: The Uses and Abuses of Jihad* 2013
16. *The Project of a Viable and Sustainable Modern Islamic State* 2013
17. *The Red Sulphur and the Greatest Elixir on the Knowledge of the Secrets of Wayfaring to the King of Kings* 2015
18. *40 Hadith on sufism by Abu Abd al-Rahman al-Sulami* 2016

Interfaith Series

1. *A Common Word Between Us and You* 2009
2. *Body Count* 2009
3. *Address to H.H. Pope Benedict XVI* 2010
4. *Islam, Christianity and the Environment* 2011
5. *The First UN World Interfaith Harmony Week* 2011
6. *A Common Word Between Us and You (5-Year Anniversary Edition)* 2012
19. *Common Ground Between Islam and Buddhism* 2011

Jordan Series

1. *Address to the Jordanian Scholars Association* 2012
2. *Twenty Years of Historic Religious Initiatives based in the Hashemite Kingdom of Jordan by H.R.H. Prince Ghazi bin Muhammad bin Talal and many, many friends, 1993-2013* 2013
3. *Searching for Consensus* 2013
4. *The Challenges Facing Arab Christians Today* 2013

Jerusalem Series

1. *Why Should Muslims Visit al-Masjid al-Aqsa?* 2012
2. *On the Israeli Demand for Recognition of a 'Jewish State'* 2012
3. *Keys to Jerusalem* 2010

Made in United States
North Haven, CT
21 July 2024

55259285R00057